Animals I See at the Zoo

PEACOCKS

by Kathleen Pohl

Reading consultant: Susan Nations, M.Ed., author/literacy coach/
consultant in literacy development

WEEKLY READER®
PUBLISHING

Please visit our web site at: www.garethstevens.com
For a free color catalog describing our list of high-quality
books, call 1-800-542-2595 (USA) or 1-800-387-3178 (Canada).

Library of Congress Cataloging-in-Publication Data

Pohl, Kathleen.
    Peacocks / Kathleen Pohl.
       p. cm. — (Animals I see at the zoo)
    Includes bibliographical references and index.
    ISBN 978-0-8368-8221-6 (lib. bdg.)
    ISBN 978-0-8368-8228-5 (softcover)
    1. Peafowl—Juvenile literature. I. Title.
QL696.G27P65   2008
598.6'258—dc22   2007006041

This edition first published in 2008 by
Weekly Reader® Books
An imprint of Gareth Stevens Publishing
1 Reader's Digest Road
Pleasantville, NY 10570-7000 USA

Editor: Dorothy L. Gibbs
Art direction: Tammy West
Graphic designer: Charlie Dahl
Photo research: Diane Laska-Swanke

Photo credits: Cover, p. 5 © James P. Rowan; title, p. 9 © Photos.com; p. 7 © Michael
Melford/National Geographic Image Collection; p. 11.© Adam Jones/Visuals Unlimited;
p. 13 © Larry Michael/naturepl.com; p. 15 © Glenn Oliver/Visuals Unlimited; p. 17 © Renee
Purse/Photo Researchers, Inc.; p. 19 © Art Wolfe/Photo Researchers, Inc.; p. 21 © William
Weber/Visuals Unlimited

Printed in the United States of America

1 2 3 4 5 6 7 8 9 11 10 09 08 07

Note to Educators and Parents

Reading is such an exciting adventure for young children! They are beginning to integrate their oral language skills with written language. To encourage children along the path to early literacy, books must be colorful, engaging, and interesting; they should invite the young reader to explore both the print and the pictures.

The *Animals I See at the Zoo* series is designed to help children read about the fascinating animals they might see at a zoo. In each book, young readers will learn interesting facts about the featured animal.

Each book is specially designed to support the young reader in the reading process. The familiar topics are appealing to young children and invite them to read — and re-read — again and again. The full-color photographs and enhanced text further support the student during the reading process.

In addition to serving as wonderful picture books in schools, libraries, homes, and other places where children learn to love reading, these books are specifically intended to be read within an instructional guided reading group. This small group setting allows beginning readers to work with a fluent adult model as they make meaning from the text. After children develop fluency with the text and content, the books can be read independently. Children and adults alike will find these books supportive, engaging, and fun!

— Susan Nations, M.Ed., author, literacy coach, and consultant in literacy development

I like to go to
the zoo. I see
peacocks at
the zoo.

Peacocks are big birds with pretty tail feathers.

tail feathers

They spread out
their tail feathers
like **fancy** fans.

Do you see lots of eyes? A peacock's tail feathers have large spots on them. The spots look like eyes!

eyespots

Look at all the bright colors — blue and green and gold! They **sparkle** in the sunlight.

When a peacock closes its fan, the long feathers drag on the ground!

Peacocks spend most of the day on the ground. They eat grain, bugs, and berries.

At night, they fly into trees to sleep.

I like to see
peacocks at the
zoo. Do you?

Glossary

drag — to trail, or follow, behind

fancy — colorful and decorative

grain — the small seeds of cereal plants such as corn or wheat

peacocks — big birds that are known for their long, colorful tail feathers

sparkle — to shine with sparks of light, like glitter

For More Information

Books

Berman, Ruth. *Peacocks*. Minneapolis: Lerner, 1996.

Scheunemann, Pam. *Peacock Fan*. Edina, Minnesota: ABDO, SandCastle, 2006.

Underwood, Deborah. *Colorful Peacocks*. Minneapolis: Lerner, 2006.

Web Site

Enchanted Learning Animals to Paint Online: Peafowl (Peacocks and Peahens)

www.enchantedlearning.com/paint/subjects/birds/printouts/Peafowlprintout.shtml

Color a peacock right on your computer screen and learn some fun facts about peacocks.

Publisher's note to educators and parents: Our editors have carefully reviewed this Web site to ensure that it is suitable for children. Many Web sites change frequently, however, and we cannot guarantee that a site's future contents will continue to meet our high standards of quality and educational value. Be advised that children should be closely supervised whenever they access the Internet.

Index

About the Author

Kathleen Pohl has written and edited many children's books, including animal tales, rhyming books, retold classics, and the forty-book series *Nature Close-Ups*. Most recently, she authored the Weekly Reader® leveled reader series *Let's Read About Animals* and *Where People Work*. She also served for many years as top editor of *Taste of Home* and *Country Woman* magazines. She and her husband, Bruce, share their home in the beautiful Wisconsin woods with six goats, a llama, and all kinds of wonderful woodland creatures.